Six Keys to Six Figure Hairstyling

Unlock Your Potential to Create a Six Figure Income Behind the Chair

Kate Hall & Chris Hall

Copyright © 2014 Hair By Kate Inc.

Printed in the USA

ISBN-13: 978-0-692-21762-7

COPYRIGHT, LEGAL NOTICE AND DISCLAIMER:

This publication is protected under the US Copyright Act of 1976 and all other applicable international, federal, state and local laws, and all rights are reserved, including resale rights: you are not allowed to give or sell this book to anyone else.

Please note that much of this publication is based on personal experience and anecdotal evidence. Although the authors have made every reasonable attempt to achieve complete accuracy of the content in this book, they assume no responsibility for errors or omissions. Also, you should use this information as you see fit, and at your own risk. Your particular situation may not be exactly suited to the examples illustrated here; in fact, it's likely that they won't be the same, and you should adjust your use of the information and recommendations accordingly.

Any trademarks, service marks, product names or named features are assumed to be the property of their respective owners, and are used only for reference. There is no implied endorsement if we use one of these terms.

Nothing in this book is intended to replace common sense, legal, medical or other professional advice, and is meant to inform and entertain the reader.

CONTENTS

Introduction... Pg 1
   Reality Check................................... Pg 3
   Learn From Experience..................... Pg 5
First Key: Prebook Every Client.......... Pg 10
Second Key: Track Your Business...... Pg 13
   Tracking Over Goal Setting............... Pg 13
   Business Performance Data.............. Pg 15
   Goal Setting..................................... Pg 16
   Reward Your Progress...................... Pg 17
   Using Tracking Software.................. Pg 20
Third Key: Education............................ Pg 22
   All Hairstylists Aren't Created Equal. Pg 22
   Address Your Educational Gaps........ Pg 23
   Salon Sponsored Education.............. Pg 25
   Am. Board Of Certified Haircolorists Pg 28
   Education As A Marketing Tool........ Pg 31
Fourth Key: A Professional Persona.... Pg 33
   Appearance...................................... Pg 33
   Client Relationships......................... Pg 36
   They Don't Care About Your Drama. Pg 37
   Ya Gotta Stay Positive...................... Pg 38
   Establish A Standard Of Conduct...... Pg 39
   The Attitude Of Gratitude................. Pg 41
   We Are Not Trained Psychologists... Pg 45

Negative Energy In The Salon........... Pg 50
Fifth Key: Market Yourself................ Pg 53
  Business Cards........................... Pg 53
  How Did Your Clients Find You?..... Pg 54
  Great Referral Plan = Great Income. Pg 55
  Anatomy Of A Top Referrer............. Pg 58
  The Referral Tree............................ Pg 59
  Discounts Lower Your Value........... Pg 61
  Tips From Kate................................ Pg 63
  The Client Value List...................... Pg 64
  Getting The Most Out Of Walk Ins... Pg 70
  Sell Them On Your Great Service..... Pg 70
  Sell Them On Retail........................ Pg 72
  Retail Tips From Kate...................... Pg 75
  Your Professional Introduction......... Pg 75
  Your Unique Selling Proposition....... Pg 77
  Networking...................................... Pg 81
  Elements Of A Good Advertisement. Pg 86
  Direct Mail – Postcards.................... Pg 89
  Ecommerce – Online Marketing........ Pg 91
Sixth Key: Time for Bookkeeping........ Pg 96
  Backup Your Data........................... Pg 98
  Time To Get To Work..................... Pg 99
  About The Authors......................... Pg 100

ACKNOWLEDGMENTS

We would like to thank Michael Cole for his ground breaking emphasis on hairstyling as a business.

We'd also like to thank Andre Nizetich and the American Board of Certified Haircolorists for establishing a new level of education, mastery and professionalism in haircoloring.

We'd like to say thanks to ABCH educator Mary Petillo for a helping hand.

We'd like to thank the good people at www.collegesanddegrees.com for their research into licensing requirements.

We'd like to thank all of the stylists and educators out there who are sharing their best practices with each other and are working hard to bring the professional standards of our industry to new heights.

Finally we would like to thank all of Kate's clients over the years who have taught us what's really important behind the chair.

INTRODUCTION

Hairstyling is a craft. Make no mistake about it. But if you want to get paid well for doing it, you need to approach it in equal terms as a business. Over the years, we've known quite a few stylists and very few say they've been given an adequate business education.

Schools want to make sure you pass the licensing requirements in your state so in the limited amount of time they have, they need to focus on the topics you'll be tested on in the licensing exam.

The exam is primarily to ensure public safety and a minimum level of competence. This unfortunately does not leave schools enough time to cover the important business elements of a financially successful hairstyling career.

We want "Six Keys To Six Figure Hairstyling", to empower women and men who have had little or no business experience along with their formal hairstyling education.

Regarding the title of our book, in almost every business there are some universal things you must do to be successful. Some keys to success. If you don't do these things, the odds of reaching your

Introduction

goals go way down, no matter how hard you try. While there are many other crucial elements involved in a successful hairstyling career, a commitment to turning these Six Keys into habits will change the path you're on and the results you get.

The Six Keys are universal steps so we know this is not the first time many of you have heard of these concepts. There is however a huge difference between hearing about something and getting motivated to actually make it a part of your regular routine.

<u>We expect you to integrate as much of this book as you can into what you do everyday.</u> That's how you make a real difference in your life.

"Habits are like a cable. We weave a strand of it everyday and soon it cannot be broken." ~ Horace Mann

The Six Keys are not presented in order of importance. The Prebooking chapter is up front because implementing this step is easy and can boost your business right away.

The more of this book you work into your regular routines, the more likely you are to make serious money. That's why it's important to study and revisit each of these concepts until they <u>become a</u>

part of the way you think.

We're going to ask you to work a little smarter and a little harder. We're going to ask you to find a little more time to work on your business than you may be spending right now. We know that's a challenge, but in return we expect your business to grow, we expect you to make more money and we expect you'll enjoy your job more than ever as you become a successful six figure hairstylist.

Reality Check

Each year, beauty and hairstyling schools are graduating an incredible number of stylists that are coming into our business. These private schools, in order to make as much money as possible want to graduate as many students as they can.

The business of hairstyling already has an image problem in that it is often seen as a part-time job or a hobby instead of a profession. Due to the lack of a solid business education and to the surprising difference in licensing requirements from state to state, many new licensees are coming into the salons with significant learning gaps.

That means it'll be less common to know what a real professional cosmetologist or hairstylist looks and acts like, for both salon clients and younger stylists trying to figure it all out.

Introduction

The good news is there will always be a market for those who carry themselves like professionals and deliver a level of service that can't be matched by amateurs.

If you make the effort to put yourself in this professional category, hairstyling can be emotionally fulfilling and financially very lucrative. If you do this right, it's a great job! A career in hairstyling can really be an amazing experience:

- You get to work with different clients every day, while you still have the camaraderie of the other stylists in the salon.
- You get to make people feel good about themselves and that's huge. The human touch is powerful.
- You have the privilege of being paid for your creativity. That's rare. Ask other artists!
- Your service is needed by pretty much everyone, and for their entire lives.
- You get to know your clients in a very unique way. So few people get to spend as much time as we do in a one-on-one situation with another person in our fast paced world.
- Once you have "sold" a client, they will often continue coming to you for years. That

repeat business is another golden quality of this profession.
- Many of you are able to set your own hours. Not a lot of people get to do that.
- You don't have the expenses of many other small business models.
- For booth renters, you make the big decisions as to how you run your business. You don't have someone else telling you how to do it. Then when you are successful, you have the extreme satisfaction of knowing you have accomplished this on your own terms.

How many other people can make a list this long? Not many. Every year at Christmas, I'm humbled by the number and quality of gifts I receive from my clients. This generous outpouring reminds me again how important we really are and that what we do goes way beyond improving physical appearance.

Learn From Experience

The people in the best position to help you reach six figures are those who have done it themselves. As this book is being written, Kate is well on her way to yet another year making over $100,000 in service and retail as an independent booth rent stylist.

Introduction

When it comes to Kate's six figures, this is strictly income from behind the chair, not money from any other income stream. While many people think in order to make six figures you have to own a salon, Kate has proven you can make a great living behind the chair, so that'll be the focus of our book.

Who's This Book For?

This book is great for people just coming out of school who desperately need a business education to compliment their hairstyling education. While this book is written from the perspective of an independent contractor or booth rental situation, these Keys can be life-changing for all stylists.

It's for booth rental stylists who feel stuck where they are and would like to jump start their business, or get really serious about it for the first time. It's for Moms coming back into the workplace who want to get back in their business groove.

This book is for people who understand they need to do more than good hair. It's for people who realize they have to take ACTION to see change. If you want this to be your profession, treat it like one and learn the *business* end of hairstyling.

When we speak about six figures, we're talking

about gross income, not take home pay. Naturally, six figures will be easier to achieve in some locations than others and goal numbers will look different for commission stylists compared to booth renters, but each stylist should strive to make the most of their situation. This book is here to help you do that.

Who Should NOT Read This Book

This book is not for people who read to get enthused, but refuse to do anything differently today than they did yesterday. It's not for people who think they can read through a book like this once and become successful. You cannot go over this kind of information one time and know it well enough to implement in a professional setting.

<u>You have to spend time working on these concepts.</u> Otherwise, put this book down until you're ready. You'll just be adding to your sense of frustration and disappointment if you don't.

We don't want to be one of the people Michael Cole (more about Mr. Cole later) calls "the waiters". These are people who wait on walk-ins, they wait in the backroom, they wait for the owner to advertise, they wait for someone to provide education in the salon. This is not the book or business for you if you're a waiter.

Introduction

<u>There usually comes a point for everyone, when they realize that no one else is going to make this change for them.</u> No one is going to be there to celebrate your first moves to change your professional life. This is an intensely personal journey. This is your journey. Don't "wait" on someone else to get it started.

"Even if you're on the right track, you'll get run over if you just sit there." ~ Will Rogers !

If it sounds like work, think of it more as an opportunity. It gets fun in a hurry once you start seeing the success of your efforts. Once you gain some momentum, it's so much easier to keep working on yourself.

The Six Keys are meant to be STUDIED. We want you to read this book from front to back *at least* two to three times, not in the same sitting. Spread it out over a few days.

Then going forward make sure it's accessible. Refer back and re-read until you're sure you have the details of what we're talking about. Study each Key and make it a part of your daily work life. Focus on it until it becomes second nature.

You Can Do This

Fundamental change is NOT like flipping a switch.

It takes time to grow. You have to work on this transformation over time. The trick is to have patience and the will power to change how you do things. Change is <u>not</u> a decision, it's a COMMITMENT!

"You drown not by falling into a river, but by staying submerged in it." ~ Paolo Coehlo

FIRST KEY: PREBOOK EVERY CLIENT

On your way home from the salon tonight, take some of the cash you made today and throw it out the car window. What? You don't want to do that? But if you let a client leave the salon today without asking them to prebook (or rebook), it's the SAME THING! If you adopt this one step, you'll make more money. It IS that simple.

Let's say a first time client comes in for a haircut. After the service is complete, you walk them to the desk, take their payment and say, "Thanks for coming in, see ya next time," or "Call if you'd like to schedule another appointment". *I've heard so many stylists say these exact words.*

This client doesn't think about it until they need their hair cut again. Then instead of calling you, they call another stylist they met at a party last week. If you had prebooked them, chances are they wouldn't even think of making that other appointment.

When you were at the desk with this same client, you could have said, "To keep your hair looking great, we can schedule your next appointment in six weeks at a time that fits your schedule. The salon will call to remind you so you don't even have to remember".

A first time client who has just given you $45 for a haircut, if asked to prebook every six weeks can be good for almost $400 a year!

When you have the client in your chair, if the subject of booking appointments or appointment times comes up, that's the perfect opportunity to tell them your other clients prebook several appointments out to get their preferred time and day. Again, tell them how easy it is since the salon will call to remind them.

If they've ever had any trouble getting into see you when they want, prebooking will solve that. It can be super-effective if the front desk staff is in the habit of telling clients that prebooking is always a good idea.

Prebooking your clients ensures your income in the future! Look ahead, don't get caught flat footed without any appointments on the books. If you've got a gap at a particular time that's good for you, you can say, "Can we schedule your next appointment in 6 weeks on a Tuesday at this same time?" This is a great tool for taking control of your schedule!

If they're on the fence about booking out, it takes some pressure off when you emphasize they can

First Key: Prebook Every Client

cancel...but they WILL be on the books...which they won't be when they walk out the door...if you don't ASK. Remember:

- ➤ Prebooking makes you more money.
- ➤ Prebooking insures that 4 weeks down the road you have $XXXX.00 coming in and you can build your income from there.
- ➤ Prebooking makes client retention more likely.

SECOND KEY: TRACK THE IMPORTANT ELEMENTS OF YOUR BUSINESS

Track your progress and watch your business grow! There's no way we can emphasize this enough. When you make tracking the important elements of your business a priority, you're giving yourself the best opportunity to achieve your goal of a six figure income.

While income and expense tracking are necessary, we want to expand this concept to cover our performance and our business habits as well. While commission stylists may not have to follow as much data as independent contractors, taking charge of your business by tracking will give you that extra push you need to reach your goals and make more money.

Some commission stylists have already been exposed, via industry educators to the importance of tracking performance data. What we're asking you to do here is not new, but it is life changing *if you take it to heart and create new habits.*

Why Do We Track?

Tracking is more important than goal setting.

Second Key: Track The Important Elements Of Your Business

Science has determined that simply BY tracking, we improve behaviors. Just by spending the time with our numbers, we can make ourselves better at what we do. This information works on us in multiple ways. It makes us think about what we're doing and more importantly, what is it we WANT to be doing. By paying attention to it, you will improve!

Tracking provides the information you will use to make informed decisions about your business. So many people "guess" when it comes to big things like goal setting, income projections, marketing and decisions about expenses.

Before you set a goal, it's crucial you know where you are now and have an idea as to how quickly you can progress. This is one of the best ways to set challenging yet achievable goals.

What Do We Track?

We track the important business metrics that allow us to understand our progress, make informed financial decisions, improve our professional performance and achieve our goals.

Business Performance Data

While there are new apps everyday that are getting better and better at helping you track your business metrics, I've used a basic spreadsheet for years. Many of these categories are standard in other educational resources but the categories below represent the business performance information I currently track on a daily basis.

- New clients
- Where they came from
- Referrals
- Who referred them
- Repeat clients
- How many clients prebooked their next appointment
- Haircuts
- Chemical services (color/perms)
- Cash
- Checks
- Credit cards
- Service dollars
- Discounts
- Tips
- Total service dollars
- Hours worked
- Average service ticket
- Prebook percentage
- Retail sales
- Retail commission from sales

As I watch these numbers over time, I get so much insight as to what's going well for me and where I can improve. It just makes it easier to grow and to get better.

You can't hardly look at these numbers without thinking about ways you can improve. And just as importantly, it makes your victories clear. Now those you need to celebrate!

Tracking is a key element in developing confidence. Everyone talks about the need for confidence. Recent studies have shown when it comes to success in business, confidence is more important than competence. On the flip side, a lack of confidence is often seen as a lack of competence.

We're not waiting for someone to pat us on the back and tell us what we want to hear. By setting and achieving goals, over time you will build a deep and visible confidence. It's one of the best ways to get yourself to *believe in you.*

Performance and Goal Setting

Once you've tracked a performance "target" for a time (could be daily sales, new clients, prebooking percentage, etc.), you're in a position to define an achievable goal. Each goal should be defined specifically and include a time frame to achieve it based on what you've learned from tracking.

Write down your goal where you'll see it. As we mentioned in the introduction, for larger goals, break your progress up into bite sized pieces. Give yourself some stepping stones. Don't make each step too large. <u>The goal is to set yourself up for success.</u>

Reward And Acknowledge Your Progress

To change yourself, it's important to acknowledge your progress. A crucial part of making this work is to reward yourself when you accomplish these smaller steps. You need to have a larger reward for larger goals, but treat yourself to a little something each time you achieve a "step". It doesn't have to be anything big, in fact it shouldn't be.

Before you start, brainstorm and come up with several small things that can be rewards when you achieve a step. When you break your challenge up into steps, write each one down and the reward you're going to get. Don't forget to think of a larger reward for completing the entire task. This is a really fun exercise!

Don't get lazy here, take the reward once you've earned it. If it's lunch at a fun place, some time to yourself with a good book, playing a game with the kids or a giving yourself permission to sleep in, it's important to make time for the reward.

These smaller successes build momentum each time you accomplish a step. You start to believe in your forward progress. You see yourself as someone who can set and accomplish professional goals.

Recognizing and celebrating your small victories are how you sustain the effort to achieve your larger goals. You'll come to respect yourself while you become great at this profession.

Tracking Your Expenses

Every viable business has to know what it takes in and what it spends. That means your business too. If you don't do this, you're going to keep wondering where all your profits have gone.

It's tough to explain your pricing to clients when you don't know how much money you spend providing their services. For starters, if you rent, how much does it cost you to have a client in your chair?

These numbers will be involved in making the most important decisions about your business. If you don' track this information you're flying blind.

Among other important conclusions, it gives you a concrete way to know where your business is now, how you can improve your bottom line and what you can spend to grow your business.

Expenses I track:

- Rent
- Color and product expenses
- Taxes and license fees
- Insurance which includes liability, health, etc.
- All equipment purchases
- Advertising and marketing costs
- Bank fees – maintenance and processing fees
- Other salon expenses like gifts for clients and salon personnel, client beverages, back room coffee and and any other tax deductible expenses.

This is like everything else. To get the infrastructure set up, the first couple of times you enter data you're going to wonder where you'll find this much time to keep your payments, taxes, bank accounts, client communications, marketing and other bookwork up to date. Be patient. Each one of these areas will take less and less time to maintain once you get set up and into the habit.

Using Software To Help You Track

There are now software apps available specifically for our business that make it possible to track so much of the information you'll need to make decisions and run your hairstyling or cosmetology business.

We're very cautious about making suggestions that will increase your expenses, but these tracking tools are a good idea to implement as soon as your income allows.

For these apps you typically pay a per month fee to use the software. The app I currently use for a lot of my tracking is Tapstyle. It tracks client profiles, inventory and business tracking specifically for salons.

If you aren't at this stage, as I said before, I used a spreadsheet for years and you can too. If it's necessary, write it out on paper. There's no excuse for failing to track.

Maintain A Client Database

Even though the salon may keep some of this data too, I think it's a good idea to track this client contact information so it's available to you whenever you need it.

Get this information on their first visit. It really is a must for your business. This information should be updated at least once a year. What information goes into my database?

- Contact Information - Name, address, phone number and email.
- Document cut or color details for each client, include formulations.
- Retail they purchase.
- Prebooking details. Do they typically prebook and if so, how far out? For example 4 - 6 weeks, the year?
- Consultation notes (She's growing out her bangs, she hates red).
- Conversational notes - while maintaining client confidentiality, it can be an important aide in client relations if you can also document some conversational notes about your interactions with your client (for instance, married with 3 kids).

This information will be more accurate if it's updated as soon after seeing the client as possible. Just make sure it doesn't take away from giving first class attention to your next client. Tracking is NEVER a priority over serving a client.

THIRD KEY: EDUCATION – GETTING BETTER

Our skill level must match the level of trust our customers have in us.

The leading edge of this business is constantly moving. Every hairstylist, regardless of their experience needs to keep learning <u>throughout their career</u>.

All Cosmetologists and Hairstylists Are Not Created Equal

Our survey of licensing requirements in each state point out the huge disparity in educational hours required. Some states only issue cosmetology licenses while others allow for separate hairstylist or hair designer licenses.

You can find the complete survey results at www.SixFigureHairstyling.com.

To summarize our findings: Cosmetology requirements range from 2,300 hours in Oregon, to just 1,000 hours in New York and Massachusetts. That works out to a difference of over a year of in-class instruction! Same license, just different states.

You can be a licensed hairstylist in Louisiana with just 500 hours of class time. In Maine you can get licensed if you're an apprentice for 2,500 hours with no formal classroom requirements. Wow! That's an incredible range. Some states require less than half the educational hours as others for the same licensing designation.

If you're in a state that requires fewer hours of education, that's not a knock on you. It just means it'll be easier to separate yourself from the crowd when you take advanced training and use that to market yourself.

Address Your Educational Gaps

As we've said before, for many cosmetologists and hairstylists to be successful you're going to have to compensate for a weak or non-existent business education.

Here in Colorado there are technical schools that offer programs for students yet in high school to take classes and receive a hairstyling license with a minimal amount of schooling. My assistant attended one of these schools.

On the day (just one day mind you) they were scheduled to have their "business module", the instructor was sick, so they just skipped it! My assistant had virtually NO business education of any kind before she received her hairstyling license.

As professional stylists, we need to become aware of, and fill in the deficiencies in our education, technical or business-wise. If you can begin to look at your situation objectively and acknowledge where you can do better, that makes you stronger and a lot more likely to be successful.

Some people have a tough time admitting to themselves where they're stuck or what they really need. Be strong, learn to grow. Education gives you confidence.

Is Your Hair Color Education Up To Speed?

Considering the huge difference in educational hours required depending on your location, it also appears hair color education varies a great deal from state to state. The problems can be daunting when it comes to hair color formulations and color theory. Let's be honest with ourselves here:

- How many of you are afraid of some color clients?
- How many of you are secretly afraid to change color lines?
- How many of you feel you have a limited understanding of color theory, application and formulation in general?

If Hair Color Confidence Is A Concern – Fix It!

If these questions raise red flags for you, it's OK. It's good to be clear about what you can do to get better. <u>The trick is not to accept it, but to change it.</u> Spend the time and effort to improve your skills.

"My great concern is not whether you have failed, but whether you are content with your failure." ~ Abraham Lincoln

In our opinion, The American Board of Certified Haircolorists, or ABCH provides one the most comprehensive and highest quality educational opportunities for learning hair color formulation and application available. We'll talk more about this organization in a minute.

Salon Sponsored Education

If you're salon is managed well, these classes should be relevant, well attended and frequent. Usually this type of education is "manufacturer driven". This means the educators and educational materials are provided by manufacturer's sales representatives and typically at no cost to you or your salon.

That certainly sounds like a good deal and it is in a

number of ways. On the other hand, if you count <u>only</u> on manufacturer driven education, you have to consider why these companies are spending educational dollars on <u>you</u>.

They're first and foremost teaching you about the application of their particular line of products. Let's be clear, they're in your salon for the purpose of selling you their product line. They'll spend little time teaching you something that doesn't help them sell their inventory.

This is not a judgment about the ethics of manufactures, it's simply smart business for them when spending money on educators. They need to make sure the expense of educating you results in profits for their company.

You can't help but notice that different manufacturers use different definitions for everything from techniques to color levels. There's a reason for that. Once you learn and get comfortable with their system, you're less likely to make a change if it's too hard to compare lines.

There IS important educational opportunities at these classes and events. They are worthwhile to attend. Just remember that stylists who <u>only</u> get their continuing education from people who make products may never learn general color concepts that would give them command across color lines.

It would also equip them to be successful with difficult color corrections that many under-educated colorists are too afraid to try.

Educational Events and Hair Shows

You need new ideas to keep your creativity at work interesting. Stay fresh and current by attending educational events and hair shows. It feels great after attending either one. It's fun to go to work. People who survive in our profession realize you've got to avoid burnout. Education and shows are a great way to do that.

Other Educational Resources

Today's print publications and online resources are excellent ways to keep your education current, but I wanted to tell you about two of my favorites.

"A Little Off The Top" by Michael Cole

Most successful people have read a book, taken a class or worked with a mentor that changed things for them. For me it was Michael Cole. Back in 1988 I read "A Little Off The Top".

That book changed the way I treated my business and it changed my life. While this book was published several years ago, the concepts started me out on the right path and I have no doubt I owe a great deal of my success in sustaining a six figure income to this book. Thank you Mr. Cole!

The American Board of Certified Haircolorists or ABCH

The American Board of Certified Haircolorists is one of the most important educational forces in the industry. Founded by Andre Nizetich, he has established an educational gold standard for hair color formulation and application. He has also published an incredible array of independent test results of popular salon and over-the-counter products. Mr. Nizetich has been a leader in the crusade to improve the professional standards of our industry.

The certification process conducted by his organization is comprehensive and challenging. The ABCH mission is to improve the skill level and customer perception of professional haircolorists.

This is the criteria mentioned directly in the ABCH Certificate:

"Certified Haircolorists pass examinations in chemistry, psychology and physiological aspects of haircoloring. They have verified their expertise in the state-of-the-art application techniques of

professional haircoloring. A board certified haircolorist has demonstrated skill in their ability to properly formulate."

According to Wiki Answers, there are about 684,200 cosmetologists in the US, and that doesn't include those with hairstyling and hair design licenses which some estimate to total as many as a million practicing hairstylists in the U.S.

At the time of this writing, there are 1,778 American Board Certified Haircolorists. That means *less than three tenths of a percent* of all cosmetologists, let alone hairstylists have passed this prestigious exam. What a way to distinguish yourself as a professional.

ABCH Educational Quality Control

Haircolorist.com is the main website for ABCH. Quoting from their website: *"There will be no single manufacturer involved in the development of the curriculum."* And later, *"It is the opinion of the Board of Directors that haircolor education should not come from the same individuals who are attempting to sell you haircolor."*

We appreciate the effort to keep their educational information and manufacturer test results as unbiased as possible. Kudos to Mr. Nizetich and his staff for nurturing this culture of integrity.

Third Key: Education – Getting Better

This board certification process is only for those who are willing to study hard over a considerable period of time. I suggest investing in an instructor or a mentor (I did), strictly for passing the ABCH exam.

Own The Confidence Of A Master Haircolorist

When your hair color skills are lacking, it can feel like you're operating in panic mode with some clients. You have to find someone in the back room who can help you figure out how to handle each challenge.

Being dependent on others erodes your confidence and self esteem. If you can successfully go through the certification process, it'll change that. It's such a breath of fresh air to have a true command of color formulation and application.

Help Plan Education Events In Your Salon

Each salon's approach to education can vary widely. If you're in a salon that has regular and relevant classes, that's great. Unfortunately there are quite of few stylists out there who aren't in shops that bring in educators on a regular basis.

If you find it necessary and have input, offer to be

the Education Director. Remember, you're not only helping your fellow workers, but more importantly you're ensuring you get regular educational opportunities you can use to your advantage.

Ongoing Education As A Marketing Tool

Tell your clients when you've attended a class. I've contacted clients after a product knowledge class and said, "We just had a class on xyz and when I learned about this particular styling product, I thought of you. I've written up the product(s) I think would be great for you and left it at the front desk. That way if you pop in and I'm not here, the front desk will know my recommendations for you."

This can be a powerful marketing tool when your client hears you've been thinking about them. Thinking of their best interests even when they're not around creates a bond and fosters trust.

Here's another marketing script that can work. "I took a hair cutting class last week and thought of you. This cut would be great on you with your face shape and we can customize the color too".

Use this angle in a post card or email when you haven't seen a client for a long time. You've got nothing to lose! Clients love the fact you're staying current and they love it when you think about them.

As we've been saying, in this business you need to embrace ongoing education but instead of taking the next class that comes along, be honest with yourself and think about where you need to get better and either sign up for an educational class, forum or webinar that addresses *your biggest need*.

This is important and bears repeating - <u>if you're strong enough to look realistically at your shortcomings and overcome them, this one thing will make you successful above all others.</u>

"He who looks outside, dreams. He who looks inside, awakes." ~ Carl Jung

FOURTH KEY: DEVELOP A PROFESSIONAL PERSONA

A persona is defined as, "an outward or social personality". For our purposes, we're going to define this term to mean a focus on professional appearance (how we're seen by others), and relationships (how we interact as a professional).

Appearance

"Dress for success." ~ *Vidal Sassoon*

There are a lot of stylists out there who'll give you a ton of reasons why it's okay to have a casual dress philosophy. We're telling you, along with most professional educators that dressing as a professional is an important habit you need to adopt. It's difficult to believe we need to say this, but you also need *to style your hair!*

Why would anybody want you to take charge of their appearance if you don't care about your own? Hairstyling, along with every other job in fashion is about appearance. How many high-end clothing stores have you been to where the staff is dressed casually?

Fourth Key: Develop A Professional Persona

This is your profession, embrace the keys to success. Of course you have to dress appropriately for your particular salon. A downtown metropolitan salon with a clientele all under 30 is going to have different attire than is considered appropriate for an upscale salon in suburbia.

My motto is: NEVER dress more casually than your clients. I wouldn't feel very confident if my client is dressed professionally for work and I have on shorts, flip flops and a baseball hat. That makes it seem as if I don't take my business seriously.

If you want your clients to see you as a professional, you MUST act and look like one. Dress to impress. When you dress well <u>your client expects to pay you more</u>. Read this last sentence over again, let it sink in.

Your appearance is key, not just the first time you see a client but every time. As much as all of us don't want it to matter, when we go out to the neighborhood grocery, this is where the bulk of our clients shop, right?

So as much as you'd like to let it all hang out on your days off, make sure you look like a casual professional when you're out in public and likely to see clients. You should still be able to find plenty of times in life where you can get as comfortable as you want. Most other professionals will tell you this is a requirement for them as well.

Maintaining a standard of professional appearance applies to both you, an assistant if you have one and your station. If you have an assistant, communicate clearly your expectations in this regard.

What does your station say about you? Oh yeah, it's talking alright! In a number of studies, cleanliness is sighted as the most important reason clients will leave a salon, even before customer service! Cleanliness also appears to be important to most State Boards of inspections.

Some people think their State Boards wait until they have a certain number of complaints before they audit a salon. Many states require the board to review a salon for each and every complaint. Avoid the remedial lessons and a hassle for the salon. Keep your station clean.

Appearance is more than your dress and your clean station. Your appearance involves your smile, your voice tone and your body language:

> ➤ Do you look and sound confident, ready to take control or do you look hurried and stressed?
> ➤ Are you making sure you have solid eye contact every time you see your client?

Fourth Key: Develop A Professional Persona

- Are you shaking hands, giving a hug (when appropriate), or initiating some kind of welcoming contact?
- Are you speaking clearly and loud enough for your clients to hear you the first time you say something?

And there's more to it.

Note from Chris: I believe one of Kate's unique skills is her ability to use her voice tone to calm down clients that are concerned, afraid or upset. She projects an attitude that conveys "no worries, we can fix this".

If you can handle these concerns and fears with a calm, confident voice tone and appearance, you have a great chance of developing a loyal clientele. Once you're able to solve a problem for someone, their chances of becoming a loyal and regular client skyrocket.

Appearance is more than how you look and sound, it's your attitude as well. Your appearance won't help if you don't foster the right kind of attitude for this job. We'll talk about "attitude" in a minute.

Client Relationships

It's important for you to consciously take control when your clients come into the salon. Don't be timid, you're the professional here. You choreograph their experience in the salon and you make sure the client has the kind of experience you intend.

Get ready.

They Don't Care About You and Your Drama!

It's really hard to believe how many stylists out there insist people want to know the intimate details of their life. How many stylists do you know that take the opportunity, when they have someone in their chair to gossip or relate the same things they would Facebook or tweet about in their own lives?

When you go to the doctor's office, does the doctor talk about his or her personal life? Bet not. There's a relation between the subjects we discuss with a client and their perception of us as a professional. Too many stylists don't think twice before sharing personal and sometimes sensitive information with their clients.

This is about your clients. Among other things, they're paying for your time, so when they're in your chair, they should have your undivided attention. Like there is no one else in the salon. Your clients want to talk about their hair and their lives. They want your attention.

Fourth Key: Develop A Professional Persona

Trust me on this one. This is not a time to be narcissistic. Keep the conversation on them. I really do believe this one little secret is a huge key to my success. While it's important to relate select elements of your personal life, remember the bulk of the conversation should be about your client.

The more focused on your client you become, they grow to believe you care about them and their hair care, *because that's where you're directing the conversation.*

Attention like this over a number of visits first builds trust, then loyalty. This mind set becomes a great tool in building your clientele!

Ya Gotta Stay Positive

This is a people business, so being positive is a MUST! Make sure your clients are going to have a positive experience EVERY time they see you.

"People don't care how much you know, people don't care what you say, **people really only care about how you make them feel!"** *~ Maya Angelou*

Each time I see a client, I give them a compliment. You can find something nice to say about everyone. Pretty earrings, cute top, love your shoes, you've lost weight...be energetic and positive.

I like your glasses, your shirt, jeans, boots, handbag if you needed more but you get the idea. I have clients all the time say, "That's why I love seeing you, you boost my ego every time!" People want to feel good! It's your job to make them feel that way about themselves and their hair.

Establish A Standard Of Professional Conduct

Regardless of how "on" you are today or how you're feeling, you need to have a <u>standard of conduct.</u> This is what being a professional is all about. Regardless of the situation, these standards should always apply:

- ➤ Doing the best technical job you can on every client
- ➤ Handling challenges with calm and confidence
- ➤ Making your clients feel as if doing their hair right now is exactly where you want to be
- ➤ Staying positive and upbeat
- ➤ Keeping the conversation on the client
- ➤ Making your clients feel great
- ➤ Doing all of this EVERY DAY!

Fourth Key: Develop A Professional Persona

Are you at your best everyday? Of course not! Trust me, there are many days I come to work and I'm not feeling it. Just remember on that day, when your client asks, "How are you doing?" They don't really CARE!! This is not your opportunity to launch into an account of your personal issues.

When a professional is at work, they're always doing fine (unless something is terribly out of joint), no matter how they feel, how busy they are or how challenging that last client was. As far as your clients are concerned, this is a great day and you're going to do a fantastic job on their hair.

My Dad was a very successful salesman, and when someone would ask how he was doing, his response was always positive. Usually it was, "If I was doin' any better, I'd be havin' a runaway!" Meaning if it got any better, he couldn't handle it.

I knew there were some days not everything was going well for him, but when he gave this response to someone's question about his day, he never hesitated. The thing is, I was always impressed with the <u>way</u> he said it. You <u>believed</u> he was having a wonderful day. He smiled, his tone of voice was relaxed and playful, *and people wanted to be around him.*

So what are we telling you do do here? Fake how

you feel? Put on an act? No. When my Dad gave that answer, I think he said it in a way <u>he</u> believed it. He was reminding himself of something very important every time someone asked him that question. Gratitude.

The Attitude Of Gratitude

"The greatest discovery of my age is that men can change their circumstances by changing the attitude of their mind." ~ William James

This will be amazing for your life in general if you can adopt this habit. When you're walking into the salon, think about something you're grateful for today. Here at work if possible.

- ➤ Do you have any clients you enjoy seeing that'll be coming in today?
- ➤ Do you like something in particular about the salon you work in?
- ➤ What people do you enjoy seeing that you work for or with?
- ➤ Do you have a big ticket coming in today?
- ➤ Is it a beautiful day outside?
- ➤ Are you going to do something fun after work or this weekend?

I don't care how many of these things may not be a positive for you. Focus on the ones that ARE!

Fourth Key: Develop A Professional Persona

Remind yourself how this attitude of gratitude is key in reaching your professional goals. You may not be able to reach them if you don't.

And here's the kicker. *<u>Even if you reach your goal of six figures, unless you practice gratitude, odds are you won't enjoy, appreciate or maintain that level of performance.</u>*

Without gratitude, burn out is a real factor in any business.

I heard about this little exercise, so I gave it a try. I have a "gratitude rock" I carry around in my pocket. Every time I touch the rock, I take a moment to think of something I'm grateful for.

I try to make it something new I've never thought of before. Once you get the hang of it, it's not hard to come up with new things. You just make a little change in the way you look at life.

And it changed my life, for awhile. But over time I got busy, I still thought I was being pretty grateful, but I didn't spend time thinking about <u>specific</u> things that were working in my life. I quit carrying my rock around.

After a while, I started to realize if I don't stop, take a moment each day and say to myself in a concrete way, "I am grateful for XY&Z", I get out of the habit of seeing the specific things that are such gifts in my life, and before long, I've fallen out of balance in my view of the world and my place in it. I spend time grinding on fears and things I can't change. Gratitude is a great antidote.

Change Your Mind And Your Emotions Will Follow

When a professional is having a bad day, they take hold of themselves and make sure they're giving their clients a positive experience and great service, regardless of their personal ups and downs.

When you start to do this, something really cool happens. You actually DO start feeling better. You're changing your focus and you're literally changing the way you feel, what you're saying to yourself.

That doesn't always mean whatever is stressing you will be solved or gone, but it means you can compartmentalize your thinking so you're not obsessed with and ruled by challenges in your life while you're providing professional services. There will be an appropriate time to address your life issues but the salon is NOT the place.

So when you're in a negative frame of mind, take some time for gratitude and a lot of times it helps.

Be specific and make gratitude a part of every day. It's a habit worth building.

"There is something admirable, something inspiring, something soul-stirring about a person who displays coolness and courage under extremely trying circumstances. A good temper is not only a business asset. It is the secret of health." ~ Bertie Charles Forbes

The Sensitive Side Of Our Work

We're in a business where some clients will see us over a period of years. Many will tell us sensitive details of their life.

I know many of you have dealt with the same situations. Kate has long-time clients that have gone through the cancer experience. So many heart wrenching moments and clients that have asked Kate to help them through their hair loss and more.

And no matter how hard she tries to stay balanced in these cases, it does affect her. Sometimes you can't help feeling another person's pain.

Hairstylists matter. What you do and how you make people feel matters. The comfort of sitting in your chair one-on-one and being touched by you can be incredibly important to your clients.

They may consider you an asset in their lives more than you know. Your clients depend on you and that's why you need to keep your professional composure through all of this.

It's important to realize you're limited in what you can do about your client's situations. Dwelling on their difficulties and taking them home with you can create a stress level that can be unhealthy. Keep your perspective.

You can't afford to take on the burdens of others. Move on from those moments and don't let your thoughts and emotions linger on things you can't change. That's why finding balance in your personal and professional life is key to your emotional well-being and to your professional persona.

Make sure you develop a life away from the salon. Learn to organize your time and remember that working 24-7 is not the formula for a long, successful career.

We Are Not Trained Psychologists

Don't get caught up thinking you're a psychologist. Listen, be empathetic but avoid giving advice. There are professionals for giving advice and that's not part of our training.

Fourth Key: Develop A Professional Persona

It's human nature to offer advice. The challenge for stylists is to listen to highly personal and at times gut wrenching stories from clients you may have had for a long time, have grown a measure of affection for, and yet you still need to keep in mind your professional role.

Resist the urge to get involved with situations you feel compelled to solve for someone. You don't know their entire situation and you never want your advice to cause any pain or damage.

Just remember your professional identity. You're the stylist, not the psychologist. By keeping this in mind, you're more likely to avoid hurting your client relationships unnecessarily.

When it comes to conversational topics, the old rule is a good one here. It's not generally wise to talk about money, politics or religion. This can affect your professional relationships. Remember why you're here. You're here to make money, to grow your clientele and your career.

There are always going to be people who wind up in your chair that have a way of being very controversial with their topics and opinions. As a professional, you need to deal with these folks without creating more stress in your life.

If your client brings up a controversial topic, listen

and keep working. If they ask you a direct question, answer as professionally as you can and then gently direct the conversation to another topic.

When interacting with a client, expressing your personal opinion on a controversial subject is not a luxury most professionals have, regardless of the business they're in.

Maintaining A Professional Persona Outside Of The Salon

When it comes to professional branding, your goal should be to make your name synonymous with hairstyling excellence and outstanding customer service. You're promoting yourself in the salon in terms of being mature and reliable.

Your behavior is a part of your professional branding. If your client sees you in another environment where you're not displaying these characteristics, they may not think of you in those terms anymore.

It's important at key times to see select clients in social situations. Just be aware that in large measure, during these moments you're still "on the job" when it comes to your behavior and attitude.

Kate has done an excellent job of cultivating

friendships outside of her salon circles, both clients and fellow workers. We know this isn't easy. A lot of friends want you to do their hair. The people you get to know and want to hang out with socially may be at the salon, it's easier to hook up with them.

Just remember the salon is your place of business. If your salon relationships become more about your social life than your professional life or too much of your time is spent giving services that pay you little or nothing, it makes for a tough road to financial success.

If you can maintain a professional persona with your clients, they're more likely to see you as the professional you present yourself to be.

Bartering

First let's touch on bartering with clients. A haircut is something everyone needs. The problem is, people will want to barter with you for their services, which may not be as useful, priced the same or as frequently needed as yours.

It also gets hard when you change up the amount of money people give you for the same service. Free one time, need to charge them the next. It brings into question the value of your services.

Salon Relationships

Secondly, we have bartering with other stylists. I know of a current situation in the salon. Two stylists decided awhile back to do each other's hair as a barter agreement. Problem is, one person has her hair done more often, has a lot more hair and now it doesn't feel fair to the other party, so it creates an awkward situation between them.

We know most stylists barter their hair services with other stylists but it's important to find someone who will treat you fairly, not just the first person that asks. Kate still trades for services in the salon, but she's specific about the arrangement and is cautious about who she trades with.

Backroom Topics

It's hard to make money when you're in the back room. Unless the backroom has a positive and learning culture, make sure you're not spending too much time there. There are only two things you should be doing during work time, providing services for pay or working on a specific part of your business. That's it!

Dealing With Negative Energy In The Salon

A lot of people are pleasant and helpful, but not

Fourth Key: Develop A Professional Persona

all. There are some people who are negative, complain regularly and never talk about solutions, only problems. There are some who are emotionally hot and cold. They can be sweet until your guard is down and then they throw out something mean or hurtful.

There are some folks who like conflict and controversy. They find it exciting to get worked up. They gain power by getting others riled up.

These personality types can create daily stress and make it tough to see the incredible upside of our business. Why not look for colleagues that are positive and encouraging? You really do have a choice as to who you spend time with. If you hang out with successful, happy peers it'll make it much easier to enjoy life.

How do you handle gossiping from others? You need to check your own gossip queen at the door. When you hear a negative or counter-productive conversation among other stylists, don't comment or respond. Those aren't the types of conversations you want to encourage.

If they address you personally, as we suggested with your clients, as soon as you can, take the conversation in another direction. This way you let other stylists know you probably aren't a good candidate when they want to have one of these negative conversations.

What's one of the main topics of conversation in the backroom? The stories our clients tell us. We want to get out of the habit of sharing personal information about our clients with other salon staff.

A lot of other professions have a strict privacy policy about sharing personal information. If a story about your client leaves the salon, it can damage your credibility. Find other topics to share with your co-workers.

When you first meet someone in a professional setting, especially if you're the newbie in the salon, be respectful and pleasant with everyone but remember, you have to get to know people over time before you really know who you're dealing with. Taking it slow when developing relationships in a new salon can save you a lot of headaches.

Front Desk Staff

It's important to understand these relationships directly affect your business. Front desk professionals have to be motivated to give you their best. All situations are different but in most cases, these people take payments and communicate with YOUR clients. That means it's important to you how they treat your clients.

Fourth Key: Develop A Professional Persona

For independent contractors, reward good front desk help financially and make sure you acknowledge and respect their efforts verbally and by your actions. When you tip them, make it a decent amount.

Remember why you're doing this. Not because you're obligated to throw them a bone, make the tip a good one so they know you're sincere and the way they treat your clients is noticed and appreciated by you. Tip them for the same reason you tip anybody else. To Insure Proper Service. TIPS.

FIFTH KEY: MARKET YOURSELF

You can't depend on others to build your business for you. While walk-ins are a part of the lifeblood of the salon, you have to do more to build your clientele.

Marketing is huge, both in your investment of time and money and it's impact on the success of your business. Successful marketing will allow you to enjoy life and have the money to do it.

Along with various forms of advertising and salon promotions, you are marketing or selling yourself every moment you spend time with a client or see them out in public. You're potentially selling your services every time you tell someone about your profession.

Business Cards

Business cards are a must! Brochures and other printed media can get expensive but you've got to have business cards. On your station and in your pocket, have your business card ready to share.

Make sure the business cards at your station are where your clients can reach them easily. Let them know they're welcome to take as many as they like.

Fifth Key: Market Yourself

If people want to hand out your business cards and refer you, *make it easy for them!*

Remember to make the content of your business card effective. Cute is cute but effective makes money. Make sure all print is legible and large enough for your potential clients to read. Include all important info but don't clutter it up.

Try to print as small a run or batch as possible. It looks tacky to write updates over the top of old information on a business card so you want to be able to afford to get new cards when you change info.

Then carry your business cards with you EVERYWHERE! Introduce yourself to businesses around the salon. Learn about those businesses and leave your card(s) if you can.

How Did Your Clients Find You?

When you're running your own business, you need to be able to track your marketing dollars and know where new clients come from. Make your investment as useful as possible. This goes for ALL new clients.

You <u>have</u> to ask each client how they heard about you. Get this info when filling out their initial client contact/profile card. Then track their answer, don't commit it to memory. It becomes important data for you to use later on. This is how you determine what marketing methods are effective for you.

A Great Referral Program = A Great Income

The power of referrals and their direct relation to your long-term success cannot be overstated. To realize the potential of this form of marketing, <u>you must have an effective referral program.</u>

Kate's Referral Offer

We're going to lay out Kate's referral offer, then we'll talk about why we think it's a good one.

<u>"The best compliment I can receive is for you to refer your friends and family. When they come in, you'll receive either $20 off any retail product, $20 off your next service or $20 in cash! Thank you so much for being a huge part of my success."</u>

Breaking Down The Referral Offer

It doesn't matter what you think will motivate people to refer you. You have to find the rewards that'll make your clients take action. That's why we offer three types of rewards.

Fifth Key: Market Yourself

Drilling down on my referral offer, can you figure out why I chose $20 off retail products as the first option? If I give someone $20 off their next service or in cash, it pretty much costs me $20 in time or money.

On the other hand, when a client chooses $20 in retail products, I don't have to pay full price for that product. At my salon, I get wholesale price which is half, so that means instead of the full $20, that referral is only costing me $10! The customer gets a product valued at $20, so it's a win win.

I offer a reward or reinforcement for EACH referral. If the reward is too difficult to achieve, it won't motivate your clients.

In my referral offer, I don't do a percentage off. Studies show that dollar off incentives as opposed to a percentage off work better. People react better to a "$20 dollars in cash" incentive than to a "20% off" promotion.

Don't discount how important $20 in referral cash might be to your best clients. Cash can be a motivator, even for those who have plenty of it.
Carry a $20 bill or two with you everyday at work if you adopt this program, so you'll always have that $20 in cash to hand out immediately.

The sooner someone receives their incentive the

better it works. If someone refers you then they're not thanked or rewarded for two months, it loses almost all of it's effectiveness. It loses any kind of excitement people initially have when they think they're going to get something.

Give them their reward as soon as possible. It works in your favor to generate excitement when it comes to your referral offer.

Do what I do and send a hand written thank you to the person who refers you. Then don't forget to thank them again verbally when they come in for their next visit. Make a note in your client database if you're worried you'll forget.

We want the experience of getting the reward to do two things. One is to make them feel it was worthwhile to make the first referral. Second is get them looking forward and thinking of who would be a good candidate so they can refer you again. They literally become an important salesperson. You're grooming your sales force!

You want to discreetly make sure your clients see your referral program somewhere EACH time they come to the salon. If your referral offer is too far back in their minds, they simply won't think to mention it when talking to friends or family.

They need to have seen or heard it enough so it

will occur to them to bring up your name when anybody says anything about hair!

Anatomy Of A Top Referrer

Let me introduce you to someone very important to me.

Sue Thomas (names have been changed to protect the innocent) is one of the best clients I've ever had. Why? Does she spend the most money per visit? No. Does she come in more frequently than other clients? No.

Here's a couple of clues. She owns a dry cleaning business. She has a large social circle that's made up of people who fit into my preferred or ideal client profile, which we'll talk about in a minute.

She loves my work. She's personable and very comfortable sending others to me. She has a way of telling them about me that makes them want to come in to see what this exceptional hairstylist can do for them. I can't buy that kind of advertising!

Along with her large social circle, her contact base is quite large because of her business. When considering the referrals she's made over the years, this one client has been worth tens of thousands of dollars. <u>Let that sink in for a minute.</u>

The Referral Tree

She's worth that much because of the referral tree she's created. If your referral program works the right way, you'll get referrals from referrals. This is what we call the "referral tree", the sales multiplier.

For the purposes of this discussion, we go with a fairly popular notion that if a new client comes in for services three times, they're likely to become a regular client.

For instance, Betty comes to you on a regular basis. She told 2 people about you and they become regular clients. That means you now have 2 new clients thanks to Betty using your referral program.

Then those 2 people both refer 2 more people each, just like Betty did and now, if you can prebook and keep those 4 new people, your total will go up to *6 new clients from one person.* As we said, the sales multiplier.

With the advent of social media like Facebook, Instagram etc., the referral program can pay off exponentially there too. If someone decides to write something about their amazing hairdresser, that's just like a print ad *and* a testimonial.

If you decide to adopt a referral program similar to mine, remind your clients no matter how their friends hear about you, if those referred come in to see you, that client will receive a referral reward.

Remind them it's is not limited to one time. They can count on a reward for each referral that comes in.

Never hesitate or act miserly when it comes to handing out these rewards. You have to keep in mind how valuable it is to have one new person in your chair.

You have a chance at developing a regular client here and that can mean thousands of dollars over a period of years. $20 is a small price to pay to get a chance at a new regular client...as long as you don't de-value your services.

The Trouble With Discounts

In retail business, there are products and services. If you're selling a product and you discount the price of a handbag, you have to sell more handbags to make the same money.

But when you provide a service, you only have a limited number of hours in the day to make your income. If you decide to charge less per hour, you can't just create more hours to make up the difference.

Discounts Lower The Value Of Your Services

A longer client list doesn't matter if you're making less money. That's why you must do what you can to get new clients in the habit of paying full price for your services right from the start.

That's why we offer the referral incentive ONLY to the referrer. Each first time client pays FULL PRICE! This more than anything else establishes the value of your services.

This is one of our major problems with most referral methods out there. Anything that causes you to provide your services for less money than what you say they are worth can confuse your clients, especially the first time you do business with them.

ANYTIME you offer a discounted price, there is a subtle message to your clients saying this is all they have to pay to get this service from you. While they consciously know they're getting a deal, they start to subconsciously believe this is all they should have to pay for your expertise.

My family was in the car business and my brother explained something to me that was to have a profound impact on how I viewed marketing from

Fifth Key: Market Yourself

then on. He told me the worst thing the car industry inflicted on itself was this idea of buying a car at "invoice price vs. sticker price". Sticker price refers to the full retail price of the car. Invoice price supposedly refers to the price the dealer pays for the vehicle.

The industry made such a big sales campaign out of selling these cars at "invoice price," that paying full price for a vehicle was unheard of.

As my brother said, they had effectively convinced the buying public it wasn't very smart to pay full price. So now people don't believe ANY car is worth it's sticker price. That's a big problem.

"Deal Sites" have stubbed their toe over the same issue. Small businesses thought this was the best thing since sliced bread, at least initially. Then they realized that just by offering something one time at a steep discount *did not* cause most of the deal hunters to become regular customers.

Furthermore, after the big sale, people didn't want to pay for that same product or service unless it was steeply discounted. Jeff Gibbard of Social Media Today.com, does a great job of laying this problem out. He also picks up on the importance of rewarding the referrer, not the new client. Go to www.SixFigureHairstyling.com to learn more.

We know salons run promotions discounting services all the time and my early clientele growth came in part due to a salon promotion running at that time.

So while at strategic times you do have to offer your services for a reduced price, you must be careful how you use any kind of discount. Otherwise, it can feel like a price increase to your clients just to get your prices back up to your "full price"!

Tips From Kate

Pay attention to other stylists that may be leaving the industry all together. A fellow stylist was retiring. She liked my work and the way I treated my clients. She referred her entire client list to me! It was the single biggest boost I had to my clientele at the time.

That's why you have to understand you're marketing yourself all the time. You don't always know who can help your business. Especially if others see you're treating your clients the right way and are sincere in your efforts to get better.

Pay attention to the busiest hairstylist in the salon and copy what she or he does. Offering assistance to that person can create opportunities for you.

The Client Value List

How do you figure out who your best clients are? Look at your tracking information! We call this our "Client Value List". We are currently tracking by client:

- What service they received.
- The cost for that service including tip.
- Their number of visits per year and total dollar amount they've spent in that year.
- We figure out their per-hour worth based on service fee (plus tip), divided by hours spent providing their service.
- If they paid with credit card or cash (one costs you more than the other).
- Number of successful referrals they've given or "referral strength".
- We use a scale from 1-5 to factor in their "maintenance level", emotionally and service-wise (we'll explain).

We set up a spreadsheet to track this information. It's pretty easy to see why we want to know how much money they're giving us and for what services. You may find there are services you thought were more profitable than others but when you break it down to an hourly income, it could be different than you thought.

I track if I'm being paid cash or with a credit card. For booth renters, you're most likely paying service fees for a merchant bank account at your salon already. You may have little to do with it if your salon manager or owner takes care of that but you need to be aware that it is an expense to you, so you need to know the numbers.

These merchant banks often charge a fee for each transaction, a monthly fee and possibly additional service fees. A lot of stylists are not aware of exactly how much they pay in service fees to these banks.

An important factor in deciding how much a client is worth to you is not just how much money they give you, it's also *how many new clients they bring in*.

Referral strength is fairly straight forward. How many new clients have become regulars that they referred? If they refer you on a regular basis, you have to take into account the income you're getting from their referrals, along with their average service ticket.

What in the heck do we mean by "maintenance level"? It actually includes several elements of the client/hairstylist relationship:

> ➢ How much effort does it take to provide

Fifth Key: Market Yourself

their services?
- Do they have super thick hair down to their waist?
- Do they frequently come in and ask for services they didn't mention when booking?
- Do they cancel their appointments too often or at the last minute?
- Are they understanding if you're running a few minutes late?
- Are they usually cool if for some reason you have to reschedule their appointment?
- Do they ask for unreasonable color changes?
- Do they enjoy arguing and controversial topics?
- Do they like how you do their hair?
- Are they hard to handle in the salon? Do they bring in three screaming kids that run all over the salon each time they come in?
- How do you feel when they walk in the door?

We're lumping all of these questions together and giving them a number between one and five, but at least it gives us a chance when determining the value of a client to consider things that won't show up in the normal tracking data.

Once you have all of this information to look at from your client value list, your best clients jump right off the page! This can also be one of the biggest stress reducers for a hairstylist.

I used to fret (equally over each occurrence), when someone couldn't get in to see me or needed special attention. Now I'm able to stay calm, especially when a client that comes in twice a year is demanding to get in to see me in the next 24 hours. I used to stress over this as much as another client that might be giving me thousands of dollars every year!

Once you have this information, you can still try to get the last minute client in, but you don't need to freak out if it doesn't happen. It's highly stressful and almost impossible to keep your entire client list 100% happy at all times. It's not as hard to focus on your best clients that give you the bulk of your income.

That's not to say all of your clients aren't important, but for your business to be a success, you need to know where your income is really generated and how to prioritize your client's demands and expectations.

Reward your best clients with notes, favors or gifts *on occasion.* If you do it too much it'll lose it's importance.

Regarding Kate's best clients, while we do spend some time with them socially, we try to keep these contacts random and infrequent. This can keep you

Fifth Key: Market Yourself

from getting bogged down with regularly occurring obligations that get tough to fit in as your clientele grows.

Other Important Ways To Build Your Clientele

Michael Cole makes such a great point in his book we referenced earlier, "A Little Off The Top". He talks about the popular idea of building a glamorous clientele, but his assertion is, if you can do the difficult head of hair, if you can solve a problem, those people become your most loyal clients.

If you can handle the frizzy, curly, the bushy, the stringy and so on, you will draw a clientele that has shown they'll pay more money and are more likely to become long term clients. Thank you again Mr. Cole.

Here's a biggy and it applies mainly to independent booth renters. <u>Be available!</u> Surely we don't mean sitting for hours in the salon with nothing to do when you can go home and get so much done?

Let's be frank here. If you do hair so you can have a flexible schedule that's great. It's a wonderful profession in that sense and for part-timers BUT... it makes it much more difficult to reach the goal of a six figure income.

Not being available may be the biggest stumbling block for new booth renters. You've got to be at the salon and available...you HAVE to. You might think to yourself. "I just got a walk-in so why should I stick around when I know it may be awhile before my name comes around again?"

- The next walk-in may be asking for a service you do well and the next person in line isn't comfortable providing that service. (Tip: Get good at color corrections.)
- Because the next stylist up has an appointment already scheduled and can't take them.
- Nobody else is still hungry for business at the end of the day, walk-ins can happen 5 minutes before closing.
- Maybe your salon doesn't strictly adhere to a policy of giving walk-ins to each stylist on an equal basis. In that case, usually the stylist that's always available, positive, appreciative, low maintenance (retains happy clients without drama), and is liked by the front desk and management usually gets their fair share of walk-ins.

Make sure the front desk staff knows you're there, and be consistent. For booth renters, you need to be at the salon the same hours on the same days, *every week.*

Come to work at the salon on Mondays if it's open. There are a lot of people that like to have their hair done on Mondays but so many stylists take that day off.

How To Get The Most Out Of Walk Ins

- Again, be available
- Conduct a great first consultation
- Be professionally and technically ready to give them competent service
- Make sure your customer service is second to none
- Sell them on how great they look
- Introduce them to your retail products
- Prebook!

We're sure you've caught on by now that we don't think the word, "sales" is a dirty word. We think it's part of the fabric of what we do. And once you've "sold" someone to the point of having them in your chair, you're still not done.

Sell Them On Your Great Service

Perhaps your most important sales job is to sell them on the success of your service. On how good they look after the service is done. This is a universal technique practiced in businesses of every type.

Most of the time, as clients we shape our opinions based on how we feel <u>and the feedback we get from others.</u> You're the first person your clients will hear from when they're forming their opinion of your work. Make sure they see the best aspects of your efforts.

Talk about how well this style works or how great the color came out. Does it make them look better? How much fun will it be to wear this look? If an important event is coming up, tie the event and how great they look together. Give them confirmation, "You look great".

And don't forget to help the other stylists by giving their client's confirmation that they're getting exceptional service. Verbal praise for each other in the salon can be very powerful, not only with clients but it'll build cohesion and a positive frame of mind among the stylists as well. We're in the self-esteem business.

While this is extremely important, it can't be done in a clumsy fashion. You can't just say the words, "you look great". You have to be genuine and thoughtful.

When done properly, it's one of the most potent tools for getting your clients to prebook. The idea is to prebook at the moment they're feeling great

Fifth Key: Market Yourself

about your service and how they look.

Sell Them On Retail

Selling retail is free money. How many times when you've made a purchase, have you been asked if you want to buy something else besides what you asked for or ordered? You run into it everywhere.

Telling your clients about your retail products is the same thing! Know why other companies do it so much? It's because they make a lot more money by asking people if they need anything else. We always want to learn from what good marketers around us are doing.

- ➢ How many stylists do you know that hardly ever sell any retail?
- ➢ Do you know without looking, what retail products you carry in your salon?
- ➢ Do you ask every client if they need any shampoo or hair spray?

Whenever you get a client using products from your salon, you give them two reasons to keep coming back. Your service AND products.

Some clients will think of you when using this product at home. They might recall something you've told them about the shampoo. Whenever you get a client to think about you (in a positive way) outside the salon, you've just increased the chances they'll book again.

If you think about it, it's your job to let your clients know when their hair needs (which you're more aware of than they are), can be met with products on your retail shelves.

It's important you know what's in your retail inventory and when it applies. You can ask clients about purchasing retail at checkout, but it becomes much more effective if you introduce them to the product while they're in your chair.

Consider at what point during the service you can "educate" a client about certain products. Think in terms of *teaching* your clients about the benefits of the retail products your salon carries. You'll also get a feel from your clients as to which ones enjoy talking about products.

During the shampoo, ask them what they like about the shampoo they currently use. Like we said, this is free money.

As we all know, sometimes clients don't feel they're able to get the same "look" at home as we give them when they leave the salon. If they bring this up it's a great time to ask if they want to work with you in styling their hair so they can get it to

Fifth Key: Market Yourself

look great at home.

In the past, unless clients brought it up I hadn't taken this approach since I know some clients feel they're paying to have their hair styled by me. Now I ask my regular clients if they're satisfied with the look they're able to get at home. If not, this is the perfect opportunity to introduce them to retail products directly related to their hair type or issues they may have.

If they've said they want to help style their hair, put the styling gel or whatever, right into their hand and let them apply it (have something handy for them to wipe their hands on when done). Any time you can get a product into a prospective buyer's hands, the chance of making a sale skyrockets.

On top of it they're likely to keep using that product you introduced. The next time they come in, another sale is as easy as finding out how they liked it and if they need more. The hard part has already been done!

<u>Synergy is when the whole equals more than the sum of it's parts.</u> When you're providing great technical and customer service, a styling education, solving a hair problem using effective retail products and <u>you look like you know what you're doing</u>, the likelihood you retain and get

referred by this client goes through the roof!

Retail Tips From Kate

> ➤ Put thank you notes in your retail bags. In my notes I not only say thank you, but I let clients know I use that money to further my professional education. This is also a great place to talk about any donations you make from your retail income. Just make sure whatever you tell them is the truth.
> ➤ During holiday season, give your clients sample size gifts of retail products they can buy throughout the next year.
> ➤ Don't use products at your station that aren't available for retail sale in your salon.
> ➤ Chemical service clients tend to purchase shampoos, conditioners and reconstructors while haircut clients usually buy styling products.

Unless they've said a firm "no" in your chair, ask all of your clients *before they pass the retail area* if they need any products.

Develop Your Professional Introduction – Your Elevator Speech

Countless times during your hairstyling career, outside of the salon someone is going to ask you what you do for a living. Your answer to this question, if thought out can be an important and cost effective marketing strategy.

Scientists say our brains are hardwired to assess a situation in under 30 seconds. Even during primitive times, first impressions were used to determine if someone was a friend or foe. This remains a small part of it but we're still driven to assess another person in the first few seconds we meet.

An elevator speech, or your professional introduction is a concise explanation of what you do in the time it would take an elevator to go from the top of the building to the ground floor, approximately 20 seconds to 2 minutes (2 minutes is one slow or very tall elevator, but this is where the term originated).

Considering what we've learned over the years about first impressions, we think two minutes is way too long. In fact two to three sentences is about it. We shoot for 15-20 seconds. Chances are, your listener will have formed an opinion in *less* than those initial 15 seconds.

A lot of people come up with their elevator speech or introduction off the top of their head. They feel they know their business inside out or have been doing it for years and because of that, don't think it's necessary to craft and rehearse what they say. Or they just like being spontaneous. Either way that can be a bad formula for consistently gaining a prospective client's interest.

This is not an invitation to tell them as much as you can cram together in this time frame. Usually you would start with who you are and what you do. From there the goal of your elevator pitch is to pique their interest, influence them to remember you and what makes you special. So what does make you special?

Your Unique Selling Proposition

Let's face it, there are a lot of people out there who provide the same kind of service as we do, so what can you say when introducing yourself that would set you apart or make them want to experience your service in particular? That would be a Unique Selling Proposition or USP.

In Kate's version of the elevator speech, she uses the term, "Board Certified Haircolorist". That's a unique educational distinction she has. It sets her apart.

Brainstorm different things, try to come up with different characteristics that make you stand out. Don't get frustrated if you can't come up with something right away. Give it some time on

Fifth Key: Market Yourself

different days. It may take awhile before the best ideas occur to you. Here's a few starter ideas:

- What are your strengths as a stylist?
- Do you specialize in any particular service?
- What excites or inspires you to do hair?
- Any industry recognition for you or your salon?

Write down what you're going to say. Spend time making it better. When it feels right and sounds good to you over a period of days, commit it to memory. Practice in the mirror. If you want to get good, get a friend to role play. Role playing may seem silly but it's not. It's super effective and the best way to develop new interpersonal skills fast.

Realistically you'll have a couple versions of your introduction. One for a situation where you're specifically introducing yourself in a professional setting, usually a group of people (like networking, which we'll get to a little later), and one version for the more casual personal encounter.

Even if you don't recite it word for word in public, you'll know what you want to say so much better if you follow this process. Since this will be your main professional introduction to others, make it count!

Follow Up With Your Business Card

Each time right after you introduce yourself as a professional, if it's appropriate, hand them your card. Anytime you know ahead of time you're going to be introducing yourself, make sure you have business cards where you can get them out quickly and easily. You don't want to finish your introduction then have to fumble around looking for a card.

With an effective professional introduction or elevator speech, you can literally create opportunities to grow your business.

Professional Scripts and Outlines

There are pros and cons to memorizing a script (mostly pros). The questions we answer frequently, sometimes more than once a day or week are prime candidates for scripting. A script can also help when dealing with sensitive issues.

- First phone or in-person communication you have with a new client
- An elevator speech in response to, "What do you do?"
- The initial consultation
- Retail sales
- Prebooking
- Your pricing structure

Fifth Key: Market Yourself

- Dealing with a client who has a problem
- "Firing" a client

A memorized script makes sure you cover all of your important points. During your preparation phase, scripts can help you flesh out the best way to answer these frequent questions.

Often, when someone sits down to create a script, they realize they are, maybe for the first time, giving themselves the time to really think about this answer, and it's usually far better than anything "off the cuff".

A memorized script is great for preventing an awkward moment when you don't always know how to put something. A script makes sure you're concise. You get to the point, communicate effectively and stay on topic.

I tend to get over-involved in some detail or think some revelation I'm having at the time is worth telling them about. Usually it isn't. Sometimes instead of memorizing something word for word, you can memorize an outline of the points you want to touch upon.

After you script something out you know exactly what you're going to say and if done properly, comes off as experienced and confident. It keeps you consistent.

Regardless of how stressed or busy you are, this is a way to make sure during the hectic part of the day, you meet these important moments with the information you want to convey. It keeps you from thinking after the fact of things you wish you would've said.

There are some cons to a script. Some people have difficulty memorizing or they tend to be stressed as they try to remember exactly how to put things. Or I'm sure you've been in retail stores or situations where it's obvious someone is reading from a script or saying something over for the umpteenth time.

They speak too fast or slur their words, which can make them sound insincere and disinterested. Even if you're saying something you've said several times before, you have to be sincere and engaged with the person you're talking to.

When it comes to scripts, the bottom line is even if you don't say something word for word, there are going to be several important moments when you need to communicate efficiently and effectively. Going through the exercise of writing out your script can help you communicate like a pro.

Networking

Networking events are local professional business

Fifth Key: Market Yourself

meetings, used to introduce professionals in your area to each other (business to business), usually for the purpose of sharing and generating leads for the members of the group.

Networking is a great way to grow your clientele outside of the salon which sets you apart from most other stylists. Networking events are tailor-made for your elevator speech.

Networking or leads groups give you the opportunity for repeated practice introducing yourself and what you do. Having a presence in a networking group establishes you as a professional within your business neighborhood. Business professionals can potentially make up a large part of your clientele and become some of your best clients so they are worth this effort.

If you stick with it you can create professional relationships that can last years. When you are repeatedly exposed to other professionals, you learn more about communicating and looking like...a professional!

Some groups allow only one person from each profession to join so that can be really cool. In these groups, every new member or attendee will hear an introduction from the stylist. That's you!

Just Google something like, "Networking groups

in (your city, state, neighborhood, etc.), and you'll see lots of ways to plug into the professional community in your area. Then make arrangements to attend the next meeting. Take a step in the six figure direction!

This is the deal though. You can't attend a meeting once and expect anything to happen. You have to go regularly so the people in your group feel like they're getting to know you and that's your long term goal. When they know someone who needs a stylist, you want them to think of you.

That can't be done by attending an occasional meeting. Joining one of these groups is a longer term commitment, usually not months but years. A lot of people won't make the time commitment. They'll go once or twice and give up. Consequently they get nothing for their time spent.

Sticking with it over time is the ONLY way you'll see the maximum benefits of joining a networking group.

Buying Advertising

Especially for independent stylists, at some point there will be pressure to purchase advertising.
While this is something you need to do in your business, it's really easy to spend too much money and almost everyone whose been in business for a

Fifth Key: Market Yourself

while can tell you about bad advertising dollars they've spent.

What are bad advertising dollars? Money you spend that doesn't bring in any new clients. You MUST track to find out where your new customers are coming from so you don't keep trying advertising methods that don't work.

And when you do try something new, make it the smallest investment you can while still giving it a fair shot to work. Don't make long term commitments to pay for advertising. Don't spend money on advertisement just because someone gives you a pitch.

Unless this is a salon ad, you decide what you want to advertise and when. Make sure you have the money for it, not when the ad person throws a "deal" your way. <u>You have to learn to say, "No thank you".</u>

Don't fall for the array of promotional items advertisers will want you to buy. Pens and magnets are sold to a lot of people who are rarely able to track sales back to these investments. The trinkets are fun to have but again, shy away from strategies that don't track well.

Developing Advertising That Works

You've GOT to do more than wait for new business to walk in the door. Don't count on the salon for all of your promotional materials or advertisements.

You may think self promotion is only for booth renters but commission people should realize in addition to the marketing their salon does, they can improve their income if they add their own marketing strategy to this effort.

When we talk about your "advertisements", we're talking about salon print ads, any printed information about you or your salon on either websites, social sites, post cards, magazines, newsletters, etc. This also includes any reviews or posts you publish about your business.

While a comprehensive marketing overview is beyond the scope of this book, there are a few core marketing concepts that can be effective in promoting your business.

Marketing materials are not the place to impress people with how cute or clever your ad can be. Some ads are trying to get people to act, others are to build brand awareness. These are two completely different types of ads.

While you may want to build your brand, chances are you don't have the finances to sustain a lengthy ad campaign to make those kinds of ads useful. <u>In your ad you want someone to pick up the phone or get online and make an appointment.</u>

The Elements Of A Good Advertisement

There are lots of opinions about the best elements to include in an effective advertisement but these are some of the basic and generally accepted components of a successful ad.

- Get their attention
- If they have a need or a problem, tell them how you're going to solve it
- Explain Your Unique Selling Proposition
- Tell them if they come in, how it'll make them look and feel
- Use Testimonials
- Tell them precisely what action they need to take (a call to action)
- Make your contact info easy to read and find
- Build in urgency (call today, limited time offer, etc.)

The trick is to do this with minimal text. Remember the elevator speech? Your ad can lose it's effectiveness if there's too much text. Be short and to the point. Pique their interest. Is there any hot trend or topic in the news that might grab their attention?

An important point to emphasize in all of your advertising is something we've already talked about, your Your Unique Selling Proposition. In your advertising, tell people what makes you special at your craft. What makes you stand out from the crowd.

Anytime someone gives you a compliment in writing, save it! If they tell you something verbally, write it down. Testimonials continue to be one of the most important conversion tools (ad elements that make people buy) in advertising. A positive comment from someone else has a lot of power to influence.

Get permission in writing from those who give you testimonials to use their comments in your promotions. Only quote the most important part of the comment. Make them short and to the point. Use first names only.

Testamonials can be beneficial in two ways. People like to see their name published so while you're using their comments to get more clients, they'll tell their friends to check it out. Include testimonials on your website, the salon website, printed materials as well as Facebook and Twitter.

Your Ideal or Preferred Client

Your advertising dollars will work best if you can make the ad effective with the people out there who most look like your ideal client. The more specific you can be in creating this profile, the more effective your ad copy (the words used in your ad) will be.

You won't be able to do this exercise until you've filled in your Client Value List we referenced earlier in this chapter. Then start to create a composite of your ideal client.

Who are your best "per-hour" clients with the best maintenance level rating? Make an educated guess as to the average age of your best per-hour clients. Add to this what neighborhoods your best clients come from and any other details you can assume for your ideal client.

This is the person you'll be thinking of when you write your ad. Think about their needs and wants. What will get their attention? What kind of problems does someone in their shoes need solved? How do they want to feel? It also helps you identify neighborhoods where an ad in a local circular may be very effective.

It's a good idea for independent contractors who

booth rent to set aside money specifically for marketing expenses. Just like insurance, education and taxes, marketing will be an ongoing expense for your business so you might as well start working it into your budget. That could mean setting aside money for:

- Salon ads
- Client gifts
- Your independent ads (including post card promotions)
- Business Cards
- Materials for fundraisers.
- Website and Social Media maintenance
- Any other promotional expenses

Direct Mail Marketing

Direct mail might seem a little bit old school because of social media trends and online marketing's increasing popularity. The truth is, we think it's a huge part of building a great clientele.
Notice how much promotional mail you get in your mailbox at home. Businesses wouldn't spend that money if they didn't get sales from them.

In fact right now, you can't just send an email out of the blue to someone, the spam police will be on your trail. On the other hand, you can send as many **postcards** through the good old Post Office as you like! That's a BIG difference.

You need to start by getting the best addresses for your potential clients. For example, you may want a list of people who have recently purchased a home in your targeted zip code (get that from your Ideal Client exercise). New homeowners in your salon neighborhood can be a great place to find new clients. To find mailing lists in your area, type in the search engine, "your town, your state, mailing lists".

We think www.vistaprint.com/ is a great company. They have been providing reasonable pricing on printed promotional materials for years now. Their website makes it extremely easy to design your own promo pieces. The postcard templates are fun and easy to work with.

Some online companies who sell mailing lists will set you up with preprinted labels. Vistaprint will help you get a list or use the mailing list you have, then address your advertising pieces *and* send them out for you!

Don't forget the size and weight of your promotional items will be a factor when determining how much postage is going to cost you for a particular mailing. Postcards are generally the least expensive direct mail piece to send. Finally, just remember to understand your total cost and track your expenses as you go.

Ecommerce - Online Marketing

Online marketing will continue to have more influence over buying decisions. We're going to touch on the main media options however we realize you only have a certain amount of time in your day, so you need to spend that time effectively. Anything that doesn't draw in new clients is not worth the time you're spending.

Salon Website

If your salon has the option for you to put your sales information on their website, take advantage of any promotional opportunities the salon provides and make the most it, especially if it doesn't cost you any additional money.

Spend quality time writing whatever you're allowed to contribute. This is an important sales tool for you so don't get lazy when it's time to make sure the information out there about you is the best you can make it.

This is hard to believe, but we know stylists who have the option to put promotional information on their salon website but haven't! They'll say, "It's too hard to write something about myself, I'm embarrassed or I feel like I'm bragging."

We get those feelings but...these stylists have yet to embrace the idea they're in SALES! No one may have told you about it when you started as a stylist, but you are!

Get into the habit of being able to sell yourself. You don't want to be the person that grumbles about how few walk-ins they get, yet won't take the time to promote themselves on the salon website.

Should A Stylist Have A Website?

A good website will be one of the most specific ways to get your clients and potential clients to see you as a business professional. Having your own website (and to a lesser degree, a Facebook page), helps set you apart from the stylists that don't. It can become part of your Unique Selling Proposition.

Just this week, Kate had a new client in her chair. When Kate asked how she found her, she said, "I went to the salon website and saw your profile there. I noticed you had a website so I clicked on it. You were the only stylist that had one, it looked professional so I decided to come to you". There you have it.

Your Business Website

There are lots of website building, domain and hosting options out there at little or no cost. You can find free website templates for your site design by doing a Google search. There are companies that will put up a website for you and will host your site on their domain for free.

The catch is, you may not have much say as to how your site looks and you won't own the domain or the site. They may also put ads on your site that you have no control over.

For beginners though, free can be a great way to get started. When you get more serious about a long term marketing approach, you may want to get a domain and hosting so you have more control over your online presence.

Getting Found On The Internet

Over the last several years, more people have embraced online marketing and understand how the search engines work. Still we wanted to touch on some basic info here for those who are not familiar with this enormous marketing opportunity.

By signing up for a free Google account, you have access to several marketing tools that can help you with your website. Google analytics gives you important information about the number, type and behavior of the visitors to your site. Check out www.google.com/business/placesforbusiness/free-features/ for a great place to learn more about getting your site found in Google search. Visit www.bingplaces.com/ for doing the same thing on Bing.

Social Media

Facebook, Twitter, Linkedin and Pinterest are some of the current popular social sites available to promote your business. As we've said before, there are only so many hours in the day so you have to track carefully to understand if the time you spend on social media is generating new clients.

Professionalism And Social Media

This issue applies to all things on the web but Facebook seems to be where this problem is most common. These pages published to promote your business must be <u>strictly business pages.</u>

This is extremely important to understand that no matter if it's a website, a Facebook page or Twitter account, if you're using it to promote your business, it cannot be both personal and professional.

A lot of young people, especially if they're still in school and haven't started a profession, see social sites as a way to establish themselves personally and socially. These sites publish information about you using your name. It's hard to realize at some point, you may need to use your name to promote your business.

Be very aware of everything you put on the web. You don't want to have personal information about you published that can hurt your business. It's time to realize in this profession more than others, your name is your brand and discretion goes with the territory.

Fundraisers

Make them count. If you have input as to what events your salon will support, choose events that will draw people who fit your Ideal Client profile. Fundraisers are not a day off or a day to slack, dress down or hang with your friends. They're an important opportunity to meet future clients.

SIXTH KEY: SPEND TIME ON THE BUSINESS PART OF YOUR BUSINESS

This is a short chapter but just like prebooking, it's one of the Six Keys for a reason. Make this happen and your odds of success go up. Don't and they will go down.

I can tell you right now, if you don't create a <u>specific</u> time to sit down and do your bookwork...you won't do it, not on a regular basis and not enough to make a difference. This will be one of your biggest challenges.

Since the bookkeeping aspect of our business isn't always urgent, some people let things pile up. You're WAY better off if you can find a regular time to do your bookwork and stick to it. You can't expect to do your paperwork once every quarter, six months or whenever you think about it.

You have to keep your priorities straight. Do your financial reporting (taxes) and bill paying in a timely manner. This is imperative.

The consequences of NOT taking care of your financial reporting and payments on time can ruin your business. The penalties and increased costs associated with them will pile up and your ability to work with financial institutions (like your bank), can be damaged.

I know stylists and even salon owners who have this problem. It can get really ugly and never turns out well. On a regular and scheduled basis, you MUST spend time to:

- Document your daily service and sales.
- Keep your business banking accounts up to date.
- Document your expenses as they occur.
- Keep your performance and business tracking current.
- Pay rent and bills on time.
- File your tax papers and make those payments ON TIME!

Don't hesitate to call the IRS when you have a question. Everybody has to sooner or later. Beyond your daily tickets and sales, you may want to leave your financial tracking until you get home. This is sensitive information that's not necessarily good to share with everyone in the back room.

While it's tempting to think you'll be able to do all of this work in the backroom at the salon, unless the "culture" at your salon supports this, it can be difficult. You have to find a time and a schedule that works for you and stick to it.

Sixth Key: Spend Time On The Business Part of Your Business

Backup Your Data...Or Suffer The Consequences

NO business should operate without a regular backup strategy for all of your business information. This might seem like a pain to keep up, but if you lose something important, well that can be a <u>real</u> pain.

There are several internet options for a fee. Otherwise a good way to record your important business information is on a flash drive, re-writable DVD or re-writable CD. You can also get a safety deposit box to store backups off site.

If you choose to do it yourself, schedule a regular time to backup and make it a priority. Almost every business has experienced a time when they lost critical data. Don't be one of us who have learned only after suffering through a painful loss.

Keep It Secure

You have an ethical and legal obligation to keep all client data you use to run your business confidential. This means you must take the time to install security software on your computer or phone. Don't let the expense frighten you, some internet providers offer security software at no additional charge. Your clients have a right to expect their personal data to be protected.

You need to let people know under no circumstances will you sell or give their information to any other parties. Never send "junk" to your clients. <u>Don't use your client list for any purpose other than your cosmetology business.</u>

Time To Get To Work!

That's what we have for you right now. Don't let anybody talk you out of making this effort to grow your business. Make the time to make the change! Make it a priority.

We believe 100% that those of you who spend time adopting these Six Keys will see immediate and steady progress as you grow your business towards your goal of a six figure hairstyling income.

"Twenty years from now, you will be more disappointed by the things you didn't do than by the ones you did." ~ Mark Twain

Go to www.SixFigureHairstyling.com to learn more about building your dream business.

ABOUT THE AUTHORS

Kate Hall has been a licensed cosmetologist since 1988 working in top commission salons in the Omaha area and as an instructor for Stewart's Hairstyling School. After moving to Denver, Kate worked as a major manufacturer representative.

She then responded to the urge to get back behind the chair as a stylist in 2006. Kate passed the extremely challenging and prestigious American Board of Certified Haircolorists Exam in 2011. She continues to serve a vibrant six figure clientele.

Chris Hall - co-author, started as a brick-n-mortar retail manager. He then spent several years as a behavior modification and communication specialist in the fields of mental health and education. Chris has also managed retail websites and consulted as a search engine optimization and marketing consultant. Chris and Kate have spent the last 25 years as partners in both business and life.